Poems for Every Season

Heather Lauren

Poems for Every Season

ISBN: 9798396867574

Contents

Spring

Springtime Dream

The birds are chirping,
the world is awake.
The mid-morning sun is hot in the sky,
the ocean-hued expanse is scattered with
puffy white clouds.

Perhaps–
beyond the old wooden fence
with its missing boards and tangled ivy,
there lies a magical forest
where fairies dance and elves play.

And beyond the gray stone cottage
where my days are spent–
Is a never-ending garden full of roses,
crumbling statues,
and a resident orange cat.
Dreams float through the air
like dandelions in the breeze.

The Swan's Secret

Ethereal white swan
Drifting on a clear glass pond
She has a secret, you know
For every night
At half past twelve
Into a beautiful maiden she turns
Whirling and twirling
To an invisible, lively song.
At dawn's misty purple entrance
Her dance must cease
Back into a serene swan turns she.

The Flower Fairy

Away in a forest, a flower fairy sleeps,
Hidden away among the foliage so deep.
When the sun's yellow beams fall over the sky
The young fairy awakens with a joyful cry:
"The sun is shining; the day is warm–
Sprinkled fairy dust wishes away any storm!"
Through the leaves and over the steam
Flies the little fairy, lost in a dream.

Daisies, a haiku sequence

Bright yellow center
White petals stretching out far
Daisies bloom all over.

The field is covered
In the whimsical flowers
Such a happy sight.

Spring, a tanka

Spring wears a garland
Of daffodils, roses, ferns,
Brushing the earth with
Sunbeams and cheery birdsongs,
Painting the hills with blossoms.

Swan, a haiku

Gracefully gliding
Across a serene blue pond
Elegant white bird.

The Rose, a villanelle

The rose spreads her petals, pink and white,
Blooming on this fresh spring day,
Soaking up the sun's warm light.

Her leaves stretch outward, left and right.
Wild in the meadow near the bales of hay,
The rose spreads her petals, pink and white.

Her fragrance lingers morning to night
As she basks under the yellow ray,
Soaking up the sun's warm light.

Other flowers try with all their might,
But none are as beautiful as the rose in May.
The rose spreads her petals, pink and white.

Wild roses in bloom are a magical sight;
Forming a bush where butterflies play,
Soaking up the sun's warm light.

Under sky of blue and clouds of white,
The rose sways in a gentle way.
The rose spreads her petals, pink and white,
Soaking up the sun's warm light.

Take a moment
to pause, to reflect
to thank the trees
for their restful shade,
to appreciate the way the river
flows and meanders around
smooth, oval stones.
Pause and thank the daffodils,
the daisies, the wild roses
and the mushrooms scattered
across the forest floor.
The sparrows, the frogs,
the way beams of sunlight dance
across the lush grass.
Be still, and close your eyes
as you bask in birdsong,
gentle breeze, and warmth.

Sweet Kitty

Curled in a cozy ball,
Purring softly,
The little tabby sleeps.
Resting on a warm blanket
After a long day
Of chasing mice and
Lounging in the sun.
The sweet kitty dreams
Of happy days and treats;
Her striped tail twitches.

Lovely Day

A cotton candy sunrise
Fresh blueberry donuts
And my favorite strawberry earrings
Twirling in a floral dress
And feeling like a ray of sunshine
It's a lovely day.

Springtime

Starting anew in the fresh, warm season
Puts me in a feeling of happiness and wonder.
Real life fades into enchanting fairytales, and
I while away my days in the garden.
Nesting songbirds make their homes,
Growing lilacs spread their cheer, and
Toads and frogs peep out from trees.
Intricate butterflies that flutter by
Make spring all the more beautiful.
Every day is filled with whimsy and joy.

The Fairies' Dance

Round and round and round they twirl,
Gleaming hair of silken gold,
Bright eyes as they dance to and fro.
Acorn caps and lacy shawls,
Elves and fairies have a ball.

The fairy queen enters in a gown of petals
And a crown of flowers,
Carried by a gentle spring breeze.
Fireflies light the fairies' path
Across the ballroom of leaves and soil.

Mushrooms serve as resting spots
For weary dancers as the night goes on…

Cotton Candy Sky

Pale pink fades to blue,
A light blue like spun sugar
Sprinkled with white clouds.

Morning sun rises
Through shades of cotton candy
In the pastel sky.

The Springtime Fairies

The springtime fairies gently float in,
Into March, all pale green and golden.
Sending forth bright sun and morning dew,
Planting daffodils and daisies, too.
They gather 'round hawthorn and oaks,
Dressed in petals and green leaf cloaks,
Whispering of magical spells
And planning to grow bluebells.
The fairy folk dance around a ring
Celebrating the joy of the season spring.

Marching

The month marches in,
With its sunshine and warmth,
And strong winds trailing behind it.
Marching, marching come the frogs
The toads, and squirrels, and ladybugs.
Purple violets do appear
In March as they do every year.
Daffodils are in full bloom,
Birds are tweeting and the sky is blue.
The day is perfect for a march
Up the hill to a picnic spot.

The Arrival of Spring

With the arrival of spring,
My heart sings,
Dainty fairy bells ring,
Yellow daffodils the season brings.

Tulips bloom in colorful hues,
Rabbits hop cheerfully to and fro,
Toadstools pop up wherever they choose,
Leafy branches wave when the wind does blow.

Robins perch up high in the trees;
I rest calmly in the grass
Gazing at the butterflies and bees
And the serene pond of glass.

Sapphire is the sky, with its cottony clouds,
Strawberries grow, a wonderful thing,
And daisies gather in lively crowds.
Each year, I fall in love with spring.

April

April's day dawns bright and clear,
A wondrous, sparkling atmosphere.
Purple wisteria bloom in cheery clumps,
Chipmunks peek out from rocks and tree stumps.
A rainbow of wildflowers flourish,
Light rain showers renew and nourish.
Fields of heather, where the red grouse pecks,
Nests full of white bird eggs with baby blue specks.
Solivagant deer meander through the trees,
A hanging honeycomb is filled with bees.
These are the glories that April does bring,
When the northern hemisphere experiences spring.

Violet

She comes to the garden
In April, putting roots down
In the rich soil.
She thrives in the sun,
Flaunting her jewel-toned
Petals of purple and blue.
Even in the shade, she is vibrant,
Blooming all through spring and summer,
The violet has perennial beauty.

Marigold

Marigold's arrival on a mid-April day
Fills the garden with cheer.
Her yellow-orange petals
Are like honey and sunshine,
Her enthusiastic nature
Gives the garden new life
As she tumbles and dances,
Whimsical and familiar.

Ode to Spring

Spring, spring–what a wonderful thing!
The sky is sunny and bright blossoms are blooming.
Baby animals are found in meadows and woods;
It's the time for bouquets and freshly baked goods.
Spring, spring–it's the season of cheer!
When the world smiles and nature is held dear.

Spring, spring–what a glorious thing!
The grass is lush and the butterflies are zooming.
It's time for spring buds on the dogwoods,
And the happy feelings from our childhoods.
Spring, spring–with mornings bright and clear!
Ordinary things seem extraordinary this time of year.

When the sky fills
with clouds and turns
to a misty gray,
do not worry.
When a light rain
descends upon your corner
of the world,
simply pull on your
favorite rain boots and
jump in the puddles.

Butterfly, a haiku sequence

Floating high above
The country field of flowers
A butterfly flies.

On light yellow wings
She dips and turns and flutters–
An intricate dance.

The butterfly glides
Down, landing on a flower
Graceful as always.

Inspiring lines
Are drawn from the butterfly's
Simple elegance.

Spring is...

Spring is the wind, whispering as a gentle breeze
Spring is the sunlight, shining through the trees.

Spring is the butterfly, fluttering in the flowers
Spring is the ivy climbing up the bowers.

Spring is the toadstool, crouching like an elf
Spring is the singing robin, proud of itself.

Spring is the marigold, bold and yellow
Spring is the deer, a solitary fellow.

Spring is the time of light and glorious things
Spring is the best season Mother Nature brings!

April Flowers

Wisteria dons her fine lavender gown,
Marigold in yellow sprouts about town,
Bluebell smooths her blue frock down.

Poppy, in her vermilion, is resplendent,
Daffodil in bright yellow, so independent,
Violet wears purple with a gold pendant.

Daisy springs up in a white petal skirt,
Peony in light pink grows up from the dirt,
Pansy's reds and oranges are ever so pert.

The April flowers have gathered 'round,
In the garden they abound.

French Countryside in Spring

The sky is milky and pale,
With gentle sunlight seeping through,
Allowing the red and orange tulips to bloom,
Blooming boldly along the path,
The path that leads to the gray stone cottage
Nestled in the field between the shady oaks
And the brilliant purple lavender,
Growing bush by bush.
Vibrant green grass and warmth in the air
And wildflowers swaying by the hills and the lake,
This vast expanse of springtime
Is an idyllic place.

The Merry Month of May

May is here,
and I feel like dancing,
frolicking in a vast green field,
feeling the dandelions beneath my heels.
It's the time to pick flowers,
picnic near the lake,
celebrate the simple joys of nature
that abound from place to place.
May is perfect for tea parties,
afternoons spent reading,
and ice cold lemonade.
May is joyful and glittering,
with rosy hues of pink
scattered across the garden
as roses bloom this lovely spring.
In May, I feel happier than I ever have before!

The Artist's Garden, a sonnet
(Inspired by Claude Monet's painting "The Artist's Garden in Giverny")

Pretty irises grow along the path,
The long, russet-hued path in the garden.
Dewdrops grace flowers after a rain bath.
Their purple petals shimmer softly then.

Among the irises are willow trees
Whose drooping branches sweep languidly down.
The radiant sun shines sweetly on these
In this fairytale garden of renown.

The artist's garden inspires him much,
So he sits amongst the beautiful blooms
And paints with violets and blues, in no rush.
His brushstrokes portray the garden he grooms.

Throughout the years, this fair garden will stay
A romantic place for painting all day.

Sights and feelings
turn to thoughts,
that turn to words
scribbled hastily on a page.
The ideas just seem to overflow
as they are captured;
so much to say, so little time,
so little space, not enough words
to describe it all
and tell it all.
Stories and poems are woven:
gathering up the pieces,
putting it all to words,
and starting all over again.

–Always scripturient

A Regency Ball

She enters the ballroom,
Dressed in a gown of white,
With cheeks of rosy bloom,
A most exquisite sight.

She steps daintily through the mingling crowd
Gathered in the stately London home;
Everyone is clothed in finery, lavish and proud
And the eligible society members roam.

A burst of jaunty music–the first dance has begun!
She easily finds a partner for the quadrille,
Through a window she espies the setting sun.
Twirling with a charming earl is quite a thrill.

Merry ladies in empire waist gowns,
Gentlemen looking for ladies to court–
Tomorrow this soirée will be the talk of the town;
There will surely be lots of gossip to report.

She leaves the ball
After an exhilarating night
Filled with merriment and dancing for all;
Her smile is bright.

Summer

On a Bench
(inspired by Berthe Morisot's painting "On a Bench")

In a hidden corner of the world
tucked away in a blossoming garden
is a weather-worn bench where I sit
filled with a peaceful happiness
as golden sunbeams shine upon my
straw hat
wavy hair
summer dress.

The sun peeks hesitantly
through the creamy clouds
in the crisp morning sky.
Birds chirp, welcoming in
the new day.
Fluttery insects stretch their wings
and fly in the breeze.
In the garden, flowers tilt toward the sun,
basking in the warm golden glow.
Vines creep up the cottage walls,
and a frog makes his way through
a leftover puddle, a remnant of the midsummer storm.

Perfect Summer Day

Blue is the color
of the bold summer sky.
Not a cloud in sight–
the sun is shining with audacity.
as the world slowly crawls on.

Blonde is the shade of her hair,
spread like a fan on the lush green grass.
Her dress is spilling off the picnic blanket,
and the ants have discovered a feast.
She's looking up at the sky,
pointing out the butterflies
and wishing this could last forever.

Cream is the hue of the cardigan
that she dons as she runs away,
away through the meadow to the trees, to the forest.
Bare feet crunching over twigs and leaves
and sun-streaked hair streaming behind her.

Blue is the color
of the stream that she wades into,
journal in hand, daisies in her hair
like a fairy princess without a care.
Stepping and splashing and spinning
floral skirt flying, billowing–
If only this moment could be captured
and saved forevermore.

Summer Feelings

In June, the world is shimmery and golden
And the days stretch out endlessly,
Leaving me with an indescribable feeling
Of summer, like happiness and nostalgia,
Unfettered enthusiasm and adventurousness.
Summer feels like gingham and light blue stripes,
Singing along to Taylor Swift songs,
My dark hair in a loose braid, and
Blackberries in a bowl on the counter.
Summer feels like strawberry ice cream on hot days,
Dreams of Italy and Greece,
Straw hats and sundresses.
Summer feels like reading under a tree,
Writing stories at the table,
The cats lounging on the porch,
And the wind in my hair as I walk.
Summer feels like finding the perfect seashell,
Poring over impressionist paintings,
Drive-in movies with family,
Reading L. M. Montgomery novels outside,
And most of all, in summertime I feel
Like I can just be me, free.

Ineffable

Up before the sunrise
that strange feeling
alone
but jubilant
ready for this.

You dash out of the
large, slumbering house
and run down the well-worn path
straight to the beach
you were waiting for this.

Sunrise like an impressionist painting
(Like Monet, you decide)
green glass bottle
in your hand
filled with wishes, desperate to come true.

Here it goes–
You're standing by
the water's edge
(it's cold)
and with one final glance
at the bottle holding
scraps of paper, scribbled with
the things you hope, dream, imagine–
you toss it into the gentle waves,
wishes carried out to sea.

Summer Evenings

Still burning bright,
the sun sinks lower in the sky.
Everything is bathed
in a soft golden light.

In the upstairs window sits the cat,
gazing out as the world goes by.
Green-gold eyes peer at the garden below
and her tail swishes this way and that.

As the early June day comes to a close,
birds still sing among the honeysuckle.
Small moths emerge, bumbling about
as the sun sets and a breeze blows.

Suddenly
the word becomes
quiet.
The sky
fades
to grayscale,
the clouds
multiply.
Tree branches
sway
and birds fly
away.
Rain is inevitable,
a thunderstorm likely.
The winds pick up
And the sky wants to
burst.
But after the rainfall
comes a rainbow and sun
and you should learn
to dance
in the rain.

Summer Rain

In the morning
Half-past ten
The sky opens up
And rain falls again.

On houses' rooftops,
Heavy raindrops plop.
The clouds become darker
With each cold drop.

Along the shore,
The rain pours down
Creating a shimmering curtain,
Secluding the town.

The sea's waves grow rough
As they crash against the rocks.
The summer rain establishes
A slippery layer across the docks.

In the distance,
The lighthouse beam shines.
Comforting sailors in the storm
And glowing through the pines.

The summer rain keeps pouring down,
Inspiring coziness in a seaside town.

Trees brush the clouds
like sea-sponges dipped
in dark green paint
specifically mixed
for blotting against
a pale blue-gray
painted canvas sky.

Tortoiseshell cat, a haiku sequence

A tortoiseshell cat
In the late afternoon sun
Dozing on the bed.

Her colorful coat
Of cream, gray, and light orange
Is short, thick and soft.

Begin Again

Eyes looking out at the heavy gray sky
It's the calm before the storm
And my feet push deeper into the sand.

My hands grip the stack of paper, tied together loosely with
twine,
As I anticipate letting it go.
Somehow, this is the hardest part–
Waiting for the moment, the exact time
To set it all free
Because once it's done, there's no turning back.

I match my breathing to the crash of the waves against the
jagged rocks.
The sea is restless
And so am I.
I close my eyes–any minute now.

There is a strong gust of wind
That makes my white linen dress whip frantically
And makes my hair fall over my face.
Then, the first crash of thunder pierces the salty air
And then I know.

Suddenly, I'm standing, running, jumping
Reaching toward the stormy sky
As paper rains down and is blown out to sea, far away.
I feel free.

Begin Again, continued

I watch as the last of the pages
Are swept elsewhere by the wind
And thunder claps again.
Without realizing it, I am smiling brighter than ever
And my feet have found a rhythm.

It's over–
But it's only just begun.
Today, I decide, is the beginning of a new era.

The rain starts to fall, washing away the past
And the sand on my body.
I am overwhelmed with a sense
Of peacefulness, relief, and most of all, joy.

I run across the shore and dance
Like nobody is watching.
Like they are watching, but I don't care.
This is the moment where it all begins, again.

Summer in Italy

She sits at a small table
On a quaint terrace overlooking
The magnificent azure sea,
With its gentle, rhythmic waves.
Vivid pink and red flowers
Bend and wave along the ledge,
Lively sunflowers sprout up
From terra-cotta pots.
Her hair is wavy and salty
From the Italian seaside air,
She wears a white sundress,
She has never felt more peaceful.
Ice cold lemonade, box of chocolate,
Soft music drifting in the breeze,
The vibrant scent of lemon trees,
Under the smiling sun.

Starry Night in the Forest

Stars scattered across
A moonlit navy blue sky,
Pine trees frame the scene.

An owl's hoot rings out,
Eerie in the darkness,
The owl flies home.

Fireflies mingle,
Their light touching the dark sky
And matching the stars.

Late Afternoon Rain

Tumultuous clouds gather
In the gray summer sky.
A certain silence and stillness
Envelops the environment
As the sky prepares to
Shed a warm waterfall down to Earth.
Swaying tree branches halt,
Birds and insects hide away.
A distant thump of thunder sounds
Carrying over the woods and fields.
And then, the rain begins
Its journey down from the clouds.
The barrage of mighty little drops
Plops against windows, rooftops, trees
And welcomes in a summer breeze.
The rainfall lasts for half past an hour,
And just as quickly as it arrived,
It disappears, leaving clear blue skies.

A wave of memories
hits the rocky shoreline
along with the choppy waves
of the cold, Prussian blue sea.
This beach has held important memories–
full of joy, but also sorrow.
Secrets drift out to the ocean
like messages in glass bottles.

Fishing Boats Pass By

Around the corner and near the docks
Rough blue waves crash against the rocks.
Jolly folks picnic on the sandy beach,
Hearty foods are shared with every and each.
And fishing boats pass by.

A cold breeze cuts into the happy scene
Ruffling women's dresses and the grassy green.
Ominous gray clouds gather in the changing sky,
A seagull lets out a warning cry.
And fishing boats pass by.

As the first droplets of rain fall along the shore,
Women open their parasols, anticipating more.
In a hurry, men pull on their caps
Then they hear thunder's loud claps.
And fishing boats pass by.

The lighthouse stands tall on its rocky perch,
Its steady light shines as clouds rain and lurch.
The beachgoers pack up with astonishing speed.
Getting home, safe and dry, is all they need.
And fishing boats pass by.

The storm rages on through evening and night;
Wind's mournful howls show harbor ghosts' plight.
The fishermen dock and huddle at the inn
And in the morning, clear skies, fishing begins again.
Fishing boats pass by.

Sunlight Dances

Sunlight dances upon the green grass
Sparkling, shimmering
Giving this field of humble summer flowers
An ethereal look.
Transformed into a golden haven
Where pixies play and fairies frolic.
The sky is cornflower blue
With impossibly fluffy clouds
You could float away on.
Everything is seen through a filter:
Light, bright, and soft at the edges.
Summer roses, simple daisies, proud tulips
All bask in the afternoon glow.
These summer days are as fleeting
As the butterflies that flutter by.

Late July

The sun, golden and magnificent,
Glows down upon the Earth
Heating the air, bathing the land
In a warm yellow hue.
Flowers keep up hope
For a late summer rain,
One that sends down a sheet
Of blue-gray pelting drops
And soaks into the soil, plop by plop.
Bugs buzz, crawl, and flutter
On their merry little way.
The clear blue sky gazes down
Nary a cloud in sight.
Deep in the pine forest,
A small stream provides
Cool water for animals, refreshing and nice.
Rabbits hop and tortoises crawl by
Past toadstools, daisies, dandelions,
Green flora in abundance.
Throughout the day, the hours slowly pass
Until evening slips the sun away
And bright stars begin to shine,
Dotting the midnight purple-blue sky
With tiny beacons of light.
Fireflies pop out in squadrons,
The wise owl hoots his call,
Signaling that night has begun to fall.

August Arrives

August rushes in
With a late evening storm.
Rain upon the windows
Announcing to all
August is here,
And prepare for fall.

The very next day
Dawns bright and balmy,
Cerulean skies for miles
And a soft breeze ruffling
The lush greenery and branches.

August has arrived!
The eighth month of our year,
Bringing in apples and thistle,
Slowly taking summer to its end.

If this merry August is cool and clear,
May autumn bring in plenty of harvest this year.

August Flies

August is passing by,
Oh-so quick
On golden wings of the dragonfly
And dandelions in the wind.
A gust of wind kicks up
Green leaves that twirl on by,
And August keeps on going
Until September arrives.

August Blooms

June has seen the clover
And wild roses grow.
July brought in the water lily,
Nettle, wort, and orchid.
August abounds with thistle,
Fluffy purple blooms
That attract humble bumble bees
And populate countryside grasses.
In August also comes the goldenrod,
Thick and bright and proud,
Creating gold-yellow patches
Along the well-worn roads.
Fields are filled with purple heather,
In the amiable month of August,
As well as red round berries–
In forests they do grow.
September, hold back your flora,
For August plants do thrive.

A little fairy,
Wearing a brown leaf dress,
Floats on a daisy
In the fresh summer wind,
Hoping to find friends.

Sunflower, a haiku

Goldenrod yellow
Standing tall over the field
Reaching toward the sky.

The Beach

Hard-packed sand
Dark tan and gritty
Cold beneath my feet.
The dark waves crash and toss
As if they are horses
Set free at last.
The tide has brought in
A plethora of shells
Which form piles and ridges
On the shore where I stand.
I stoop to sift through
These treasures from the sea:
Olive shells, lion's paws, lightning whelks
All are appreciated.
They drop into the bucket along with
Conch shells, auger shells, jingle shells.
When I leave,
Tall grass and wildflowers
Frame the pathway from the beach.

Thunderstorm

Torrents of heavy rain
Pour down from the
Ominous, gray-blue expanse
Splattering against windows
Soaking the ground.
The wind rushes and howls
Thunder booms, lightning flashes
Splitting the sky jaggedly in two.
The storm rages, then slows
Like it has let all of its
Anger and energy out of the clouds.

The Fish Pond, a haiku sequence

In a placid pond
Under a small, arching bridge
Large orange fish swim.

Koi fish swim slowly,
Making lazy loops in the
Rippling water.

The serene fish pond
Belongs to them; it is home
Framed by rocks and grass.

The Summer Fairy

The summer fairy
Slips away
In a golden cloud
Scented with rosebuds and
Decorated with daisies.
She has done all she
Needed to do,
Sprinkled the rain and
Spread the sun's rays.
The autumn fairy
Tumbles through
On a heavy cloud
Scented with cinnamon and
Decorated with orange-brown leaves.

Summer to Fall

One of my favorite
times of all
is the merry transition
from summer to fall.

Leaves start to change,
nights grow cold,
cozy sweaters are worn,
eerie stories are told.

We gather around campfires,
see bats take to the sky,
go on jolly hayrides,
and hear an owl's screeching cry.

Hang onto the last of summer
but welcome in fall gratefully,
it's time for pumpkins
and rolling in leaves playfully.

Autumn

Autumn Falls

Autumn falls into place
Like a gust of blustery wind
Like a pumpkin pie set on a table
Like the stars dotting the night sky.

Autumn sweeps in
Like a fragrant cinnamon broom
Like raking the colorful leaves
Like a specter in a spooky story.

September

Scents of cinnamon and pumpkin linger,
Everyone is preparing for autumn,
Pulling out cozy knit sweaters,
Taking time to enjoy golden afternoons.
Embers dance in the fireplace,
Mystery novels are read on rainy nights,
Baked goods create an autumnal aroma.
Every heart is warmed by apple cider and doughnuts,
Red and orange leaves fill trees.

The Pumpkin Patch

The autumnal afternoon sky
hangs over a golden-brown field
where pumpkins rest on curly vines
with leafy green hats
and sturdy brown stems.
Through the pumpkin patch
people in chunky sweaters roam
stopping to pick the perfect gourd
to grace their front doorstep
or cozy living room.
The pumpkins, sitting proudly
large and small, bumpy and smooth
in shades of tangerine and burnt orange
wait patiently to go home.
Will they be turned into jack-o'-lanterns?
Or used for pumpkin pie?
Round pumpkins are scooped up
as the sun grows lower in the sky
and then the patch closes for the night.

Autumn Morning, a haiku sequence

Misty purple sky
Over a goldenrod field
Welcoming the day.

As the sky lightens
Leaves of orange and yellow
Flutter slowly down.

The fresh air is crisp
Soft yellow sunlight shines through
Morning has arrived.

Pumpkin Field, a haiku

A gust of chill wind
Sweeps over the grassy field
Where pumpkins grow.

Bat, a haiku

On his black webbed wings
The Halloween bat takes flight
Soaring over the woods.

Jack-o'-lantern, a haiku

Big, round, and orange
Golden light shining from its
Beckoning carved face.

Beginning October

The sky is a harmony
Of purple-blue watercolors.
The sun begins its day
As I do the same.
Burnt orange sweater,
Cold feet on wood floor.
Warm cinnamon oatmeal and
An apple from the fairytale orchard,
And it's time to spread my wings.
Out the front door of my cottage
Into the vibrant setting of
This brilliant, magical autumn morning.
Through fields of golden brown I frolic,
Through woods of changing trees I walk.
The world seems to sing
A mystical elfin tune, welcoming fall.
Sweet fall blooms, black-eyed susan and thistle
Brighten nature's well-worn paths.
Wild pumpkins grow, hidden by leaves.
Toadstools and moss and pinecones
Seem to create a fairy village.
I walk on, enjoying the moment
On this October morning.

The sidewalk is a glassy mirror
Gray and blue and slick
Where orange and red leaves
Fall down from shady trees
And drop down into it.

Waiting Cat

Round, vibrant green eyes stare out
She arches her back, swishes her tail
The cat is ready to pounce.

Windy Leaves, a haiku

A swirling wind kicks
Up a gust of autumn leaves
Scattering them far.

The Pumpkin House

Welcome to the great big pumpkin house,
Where all creatures dwell, even a mouse
Where good witches play and friendly ghosts dance
Come down to the pumpkin, don't miss the chance.

Hidden away in a deep, dark wood,
The house's tenants would stay all year if they could.
Field mice, chipmunks, and grumpy gnomes
Call this large gourd home sweet home.

The pumpkin appears in September each year
And creatures arrive from far and near.
Then, in October on Halloween night
The pumpkin rolls away, out of sight.

October

Out in the golden-brown field
Crows circle in the dusky sky,
Trees whisper, dropping brittle leaves, and
Owl makes his home in a hollow.
By the light of the moon, pumpkins grow.
Eerie sounds permeate the heavy air,
Radiant is the moon on this October night.

Ode to the Halloween Pumpkin

Pumpkin, oh pumpkin,
You're quite the country bumpkin.
Sitting on top of straw so yellow,
You are a true Halloween fellow.
Oh, pumpkin, how orange and round,
Measuring two feet from top to ground.
Proudly guarding the front of our house
Scaring away any black cat, bat, and mouse.
On Halloween morning, we will give you a face
And a shining light that can be seen from anyplace.
Pumpkin, oh pumpkin,
With your candlelight grin
May you bring festive cheer,
Attracting friends from far and near.

Cold Morning in Autumn

The first morning of crisp, cool air,
And my autumnal heart sings
As the trees and their leaves
Dress in their vivid fall colors
And the wind whips in spirals,
The air like thick paint swirls.
Brown cardigan around me
Protects me from the cold,
But still I feel wind's chilly gust
As I walk briskly down the path.
The benches stand empty,
Not a bird or bug is seen.
The sky is a heavy quilt
Of blue and gray and white
And I smile, despite
The cold against my face
On this mid-October day.

Leaves waltz
a whimsical pattern
in her wake.

The wind flutters
her hair and
whispers its autumnal magic.

Her long skirt
swishes like she's
an autumn fairy princess.

The falling leaves
all around her
scatter, flutter, land.

Leaves crunch
a crinkly fall sound
in her wake.

Market Day

Bustling market with
Bursts of activity,
Noise–
A barrage of voices and sights and smells
Garlic and meat pies and cinnamon
Twisting through the air
And everybody, all at once,
Bargaining and greeting and shouting.
The creak of carts, the squawk of a hen
A travelling band strikes up a tune
Lively and frantic,
Like rough burlap, worn wood, fresh vegetables
Chaos.
Amidst it all–
Is me, who was late today
Who forgot the eggs again
Who has her own quiet worries,
Lost amongst the everyday excitement.

The Autumn Fairy

The autumn fairy sweeps
With a broom of twigs and cinnamon.
Her hair is straight and brown; she keeps
It tied back with a handkerchief,
And when September arrives, she leaps
Into action to scatter the leaves
And chill the winds, and ivy creeps
Around the walls of her dwelling.
A little stone cottage is where she sleeps,
Cooks pumpkin seeds as a fall treat.
Her wings are amber, and she keeps
Flying and spreading her magic.

November

Nestled deep in the forest,
Owls hoot a haunting tune,
Vermilion flowers grow in the thicket,
Elves seem to peek through the trees.
Mushrooms dot the forest's edge,
Birds take flight south.
Evening floats in, dusky and cold
Rambling ivy clumps and grows.

There's something about
The clear blue bright skies
Of early autumn mornings.

As the season continues,
The blue turns to gray
And cloudy dark winter sets in.

Chilly November Night

A fire in the hearth
Warms this chilly November night,
When all the house is silent
And my candle is burning bright.

I sit upon the sofa,
Wrapped in a quilt of cranberry red,
Reading a thick, worn novel
A pillow behind my head.

As I get lost between the pages,
A plate of cookies and hot tea
And the cat curled up at my feet
Bring autumnal joy and comfort to me.

Gray clouds bring in the nighttime sky,
The north wind sprinkles the stars,
The moon glows round like a beacon,
And the air grows frigid as ice.

Dusty brown leaves pave the forest floor,
Small animals burrow and rest,
Gusts of wind whisper their secrets
Into the vast and silent night.

Day slips away
Into the autumn night sky.
Dark clouds rush through
The starless expanse
And cold rain comes
Tumbling down.
Tapping at the windows,
Insistent to be let in.
Like a moth–like a ghost.
Shutter the windows, but
The house shudders
In this late November storm.

At Sea

My heart is like a yellow bird
Free from its wrought-iron cage,
Free from the depths of the moors,
As I board the ship
And stare across the ocean
Watching the sky change,
Feeling the chill dance in the air,
Pulling my wool sweater tighter
Over the scratchy green dress I wear–
The dress that held me back in its heavy fabric
When all I wanted was
To ride away on my old horse at dawn.
We are leaving the port,
Leaving behind the cloudy skies,
Howling wind, and frigid moors.
I feel free, but I remember
My old wooden trunk that holds my heart,
My heart expressed in the midnight ink
Of a feather pen, compact script,
I composed the lines that
Allowed me to fly.
Fly away did I, on shimmering wings.
I left everything in hopes of
Finding something at sea.

A drizzle of rain
Makes a regular November day,
And I set off with my umbrella.
Through dense woods I go,
Following the timeless path
Lined with toadstools and dry leaves.
My friends in the forest–
The woodpecker, the squirrel, and
The spry orange fox–
Go about their day, on their merry way.
Bramble leaves and round berries
Are perfect things to sketch,
In my little leather journal with
My handy black pen.

Ancient Oak Tree

Ancient oak tree
With its long stretching limbs
Adorned with glass bottles,
Tied with scraps of fabric,
Holding the wishes and hopes
Of ever so many.
The tree guards the secrets
Of bygone times,
Listens to all it is told.
If you listen closely,
You might just hear
The old tree's sage reply.
For every tree has a story
Hidden among its leaves.

Reading poetry
by candlelight
wrapped in an
old, faded patchwork quilt.

Everything starts to feel all right.

Sometimes,
the simplest things
are the most
comforting.

A stormy gray sky
Swirling with muted blues
        heavy clouds
        tempestuous winds
Creates the perfect backdrop
(as in an ominous nineteenth century oil painting
hanging on the wall in a grand inherited manor)
For a sprawling house
On a craggy cliff,
Teeming with mysteries and secrets.

Winter

The Winter Fairy, a haiku sequence

The autumn fairy
Gathers up her falling leaves,
Takes to flight, away.

The winter fairy
Swoops in on icy wind gusts
Sprinkling snowflakes.

She paints the sky gray,
Forms icicles on buildings,
Grows holly and ivy.

Her blustery days
And long, frigid winter nights,
We're jolly despite.

With an icy crown
She flies through the misty land,
Cape trailing after.

Leaving in her wake
An abundance of snowflakes:
Winter has arrived.

Winter's Coming

Gone away is the fall,
Picking up its tempestuous leaves
Of golden brown and orange,
Sending critters to their hideaways,
Leaving the trees swaying and bare
Stark silhouettes against a pale gray sky.
Winter is coming, bringing with it
Blasts of cold air and pounding rain,
Rain that will turn into snow and
Bury the town in a soft white blanket.

A Cup of Tea

A cup of piping hot tea
on a cold winter's night
is like a twinkling star
in the dark midnight sky.
A cozy blanket and a book
do complete this winter night,
all is calm and all
is happy and bright.

Old World Kitchen

While the snow and the cold
Come pressing down
On the world, all around,
Within a little cottage
Tucked deep in the woods
Warm memories are being made
In a grandmother's kitchen.
Red and white polka-dotted hair scarves
And long black woolen skirts
Are worn by three generations
As recipes as old as time form.
Scents of cumin, dill, and garlic,
Borscht and latkes and braised cabbage,
These hearty dishes are made by those
With warm hearts in this snowy, frozen world.
Old world aromas drift throughout
The home as songs are sung,
Telling of trees and snow and winter,
The season has now begun.

Wild Winter Wind is Calling

Wild winter wind is calling:
Come away, across the snow
Across the bridge, and through the forest.
Come away, across the sea
Through the stars, and home you'll be.
Wandering in the winter white,
Made of snow and cold as ice.

Wild winter wind is calling:
Come away, across the sky
Float like snowflakes, through the night.
Come away, across the mountains
Brave the wind and ice and frost.
Hear the sorrowful, whirling song
As the winter wind howls on and on.

Snowfall

Through the light gray sky,
Tumbling and whirling,
Tiny snowflakes arrive.
They fall slowly down,
Settling on all surfaces
Creating a pure white blanket.
Soon the snow is growing thick
Falling, falling, everywhere!
The world is covered in wintry white,
Slippery and sparkling, frigid as ice.
The morning light shines bright and soft
Illuminating the snowy landscape
Quiet, calm, and filled with peace.

December

Decorations bring good cheer,
Enlivening the holiday atmosphere.
Carols are sung on wintry nights, and
Everyone is happy, joyful, and kind.
Mistletoe, holly, and ivy grow,
Baskets of goodies bring merriment to all.
Evergreen trees are strung with lights,
Remarkable celebration time!

Figure Skating

The first puff of cold air
Seems to beckon me
As I step onto the ice.
I circle around the edge
Of the rink, drawing
Crisp ridges into the surface
Of fresh, shiny, frozen water.
Soon, the cold is no longer bitter;
It is invigorating as I skate
Round and round, growing faster.
Then it is time: I glide to the center
And begin my graceful routine.
With each stroke, turn, spin, and jump,
I feel exhilarated and
The outside world melts away.
Spinning, here, with my black skirt
Flying out around me, my ponytail
Whipping in the air, I feel like
A princess of the ice and snow.
Dancing, making my way across the icy expanse,
Forward and backwards, with
The blades of my skates gliding
Smoothly, briskly, across the ice,
I feel at home.

Christmas Night

Holiday lights are beaming,
Warm and bright.
Everyone is cozy
On this chilly winter night.
Jingle bells are ringing,
Songs make everything right.
Blankets and hot cocoa
And yellow candlelight
Makes us feel so merry
On this brilliant Christmas night.

Snowflakes, a haiku

Slowly floating down
Elegant white snowflakes shine
Bringing winter chill.

Ballet, a haiku

Spinning and twirling
Pink shoes leap gracefully up
A sea of tutus.

Cozy Cat, a haiku sequence

The black and white cat
Is quite cozy on the couch
As she looks outside.

Her green eyes gaze out
Her tail swishes to and fro
Enthralled with the world.

The Winter Fairies

Icy cold is the winter sky,
Low and gray on this January night.
When all the world is silent and calm,
The winter fairies sing their song.
Through the bare branches,
Dark shadows on the sky, they fly.
Landing in a forest all covered in snow,
The fairies' ice blue gowns sparkle and shine.
Their wings are clear and gleam like ice,
Their winter carol fills the vast, dark night.
With each verse sung,
Snowflakes scatter through the sky,
Floating and landing on all surfaces in sight.
A harsh wind blows, chilling the land.
The fairies retreat with it, riding on air.

Dance of the White Swan

On a frozen pond
The graceful swan dances,
Her feathers as white
As the fresh-fallen snow,
And eyes glittering in the
Late evening twilight.

Snow-dusted fir trees
Envelop the still, wintry lake
Where the solitary swan
Glides back and forth,
The ice as her stage
For this winter ballet.

Frozen land,
With a cold
Gray-blue sky.
The season persists,
And the dry,
Crumbling leaves
Are swept off the
Leaning old tree.
Winter descends,
Covering everything with
Its solemn, snowy layers.

The Winter Elf, a haiku

Away in a tree
The wise winter elf slumbers
As the wind roars on.

Snowflakes (2), a haiku

Dainty snowflakes fall
Gliding slowly down to Earth
Elegant and white.

Winter's Icy Coronet

Winter's icy coronet
She dons upon her head,
Her frigid waves
Of ashy blonde
Set off her sparkling jewels.
The ring of silver
Slim and cold
Built up sharply with dark blue stones
Interspersed with icicle spikes
And decorated with glittering diamonds.
As she walks, she sends forth winds,
Winds of ice and frozen lands,
With a sparkle of
Her cold coronet
Snow will fall; ponds will freeze
Hibernation beckons creatures
Folks take refuge in their homes
When cold and frigid Winter descends.
Yes, the reign of autumn
Reaches its fair end
When cold and frigid Winter descends.

The Magic of Winter

Winter carries a certain magic
Felt in the silence of early mornings,
Seen in the way pine trees dot the landscape.
A puff of chilly breath,
An old book cracked open at dusk,
Hot chocolate warming hands.
Magic presents itself in small ways
If you only stop to notice–
The purple-blue of cold, misty skies
A well-loved blanket, a purring cat.
Bright red cardinals flying high
And glittering icicles, glimmering frost.
Candle wax melting, a light in the darkness.
Just when everything seems frozen and desolate–
You realize that you've loved winter all along.

The Castle

The castle is a striking figure,
Its shadow cast down from the cliff
And flung out over the choppy sea.
The sky is the perfect backdrop
Like an oil painting of pewter and cobalt.
Within the thick stone walls,
Shadows flicker like ghosts down the corridors,
Dusty tapestries shroud the walls,
A lonely organ plays a haunting song.
The air is chilly and heavy with must
As the old castle slumbers,
Its secrets guarded by time.

February

February's days are drizzly and gray,
Enveloped in a feeling of coziness.
Brisk winds and rain no doubt appear,
Rushing into warmer months, and cheery
Umbrellas dot the streets with each
Amicable late winter rain shower.
Resplendent are these last days of cold,
Yet we yearn for sunshine and flowers.

The Library in Winter

Warmth radiates from within.
You could get lost for hours
Amongst the silent, dusty shelves
And the precious stories,
Just waiting for you to come along.

As frigid winds and freezing temperatures
Affect the outside world,
Here, you are safe,
Ensconced in a chair in a corner
With the comforting glow of a lamp
Guiding you as you read
In the library in winter.

Good-bye, faeries of the frost,
Your months of reign
Soon draw to a close,
Your wintry world
Is almost lost
To spring's sweet sunny days.
Pick up the last remnants of
Icy days and chilling nights;
Fly them far away.
Across the sea and
Back to the land
Of faerie folk, beyond the mist
Of the purple-gray sky.
Good-bye, faeries of the frost,
Come back again
When autumn days turn dark.

Winter's Letter to Spring

Dear Spring,
How I love the joy you bring.
After my dark, cold days
And mysterious snowy ways
Your lovely birdsong will ring
In warmer weather, that's the thing.

Oh, yes, Spring,
Of Decembers, Januarys, Februarys, I am the king,
But you are the queen of Marches, Aprils, Mays,
And pastel, halcyon, lighthearted days.
But I must say, my season is sparkling
Just as much as yours, happy times it does bring.

Hear me out, Spring.
I bestow snowflakes, beautiful and glittering;
Give people the chance for cozy indoor days,
And fun playing in the snow in many ways.
I have mistletoe, evergreens, and sparrows brown of wing.
Sincerely, Winter (paving the way for spring)

Winter is Melting Away

Winter is melting away.
Frozen expanses thaw,
Sunlight is beating down,
Weak at first–then brighter.
The sky does not seem
To droop as low,
With its murky gray hue
Turned cerulean blue, and
The clouds are buoyant and free.
Snow on the ground has disappeared,
Giving way to green grass
And ever-growing wildflowers.
Winter is melting away.

About the Author

Heather Lauren is a reader, writer, and lover of cats. She is a fan of Jane Austen, the Brontë sisters (Charlotte, Emily, and Anne), L.M. Montgomery, Maud Hart Lovelace, and Emily Dickinson. She is always writing stories and hopes to publish another book in the near future!

Made in the USA
Middletown, DE
12 October 2023

40706931R00066